GW01158858

Having a Healthy Mind

through the

Mind of Christ

PALMETTO
PUBLISHING
Charleston, SC
www.PalmettoPublishing.com

© 2024 by Charles E. Boyce

All rights reserved.

Paperback ISBN: 9798822962569
eBook ISBN: 9798822962576

Charles E. Boyce

Having a
Healthy Mind
through the
Mind of
Christ

CONTENTS

AUTHOR BIO

Pastor Charles Boyce is 55 years old and has been involved in ministry for 36 years. Charles accepted Jesus Christ as his personal Lord and Savior on June 4, 1988 when he was 19 years old. While working at a Boy Scout camp in Bonner Springs, Kansas, a Baptist minister, Eddie Wakes, befriended Charles and shared the gospel with him. It was from that moment the Lord gave Charles a love for the word of God and a desire to be used of him. It has been that love and desire that has motivated Charles throughout his adult life.

On January 22, 1989, Charles became a licensed minister of the gospel at Oak Ridge Missionary Baptist Church in Kansas City, Kansas. From 1990 to 1994, both Charles and his wife of 34 years, Trish, were members of Kansas City Baptist Temple. It was during this time that both Charles and Trish were trained in discipleship and attended the church's four-year pastor's school of ministry. Through the years they had the privilege of doing discipleship conferences in various churches in the United States, including a mission trip to Romania in 1991. In 1994 Charles and Trish graduated from pastor's school and Charles was ordained to minister the word in Ontario, Canada. Charles, Trish, and their young son at the time, Andrew, moved and lived outside of the Toronto area for seven and a half years. During that time they ministered in Graceway Baptist Church for three years before starting Victory Bible Church. While in Canada Charles developed a ministry among Halton Police Services and even became a volunteer police officer. Charles also started and co-hosted a local cable teen talk show in order for police to gain further insight on issues teens deal with daily.

Since moving back to the Kansas City (KC) area in 2002, Charles continued to minister the word in the KC area and then worked with Pastor David Davis to start Kansas City Bible Church in 2005. Charles served as the children's pastor and then later as the young adult pastor before moving to Southeast Kansas to start Faith Bible Church in 2016 where he serves as a senior pastor today.

Charles also graduated from The University of Missouri in Kansas City in 1992 with a Bachelor's of Arts degree in Sociology. He has continued to train in karate for over 35 years and holds the rank of sixth degree black belt. At one time he owned and operated six dojos in the Kansas City Metro Area. Charles has been involved in law enforcement both in Canada and in the state of Kansas over the last 25 years as a volunteer, chaplain, and patrol officer. He currently works as an enforcement agent for Kansas Racing and Gaming Commission (KRGC). With this extensive background, Charles has a unique perspective in the need of mental health.

ACKNOWLEDGMENTS

To My Lord
Without my Lord and Savior Jesus Christ, I have no life or purpose. I thank him for my salvation and giving me purpose in this life.

Ephesians 2:10 KJV
For we are his workmanship, created in Christ Jesus unto good works, which God hath before ordained that we should walk in them.

To My Wife, Trish Boyce
There is no way that I could do anything in ministry over the last 34 years without my incredible wife, Trish Boyce. The Lord provided me a great helpmeet in ministry.

Proverbs 31:10-12 KJV
Who can find a virtuous woman? for her price is far above rubies. [11] The heart of her husband doth safely trust in her, so that he shall have no need of spoil. [12] She will do him good and not evil all the days of her life.

To My Son, Andrew Boyce

So thankful to the Lord that he gave us you for our only son and child. I have learned so much from you as you grew up in our house and even more so from you as a young adult. I love your perspective and the insight you give me in the word of God.

1 Timothy 1:2 KJV
Unto Timothy, my own son in the faith: Grace, mercy, and peace, from God our Father and Jesus Christ our Lord.

To My Fellow Laborers in Ministry

David Davis

It has been a privilege to work with you through the years in ministry. So thankful to the Lord to minister under you at Kansas City Bible Church where I learned from you more extensively on how to rightly divide the word of truth.

Curt Courtney

I am so thankful that Trish and I have you and your wife, Pam, to labor together in ministry at Faith Bible Church. I can't imagine doing this work without you guys alongside us.

Sam Okiror

To my newfound brother in Christ doing the work of the ministry in Uganda, Africa. You are an inspiration to me, and seeing your diligence in writing a commentary on the book of Romans has given me the needed push to write this work.

1 Thessalonians 3:2 KJV
And sent Timotheus, our brother, and minister of God, and our

fellowlabourer in the gospel of Christ, to establish you, and to comfort you concerning your faith:.

All scripture references are from the King James Version.

INTRODUCTION

When I was a child growing up in the '70s, I remembered a commercial on TV focused on African Americans going to college to further their education. These commercials always ended with the following statement, "A mind is a terrible thing to waste." This slogan was developed by Forest Long of Young & Rubicam in partnership with the Ad Council for the United Negro College Fund (UNCF).

This slogan is true spiritually as well. Too many Christians waste the mind that has been given them in Christ. Even among believers in Christ, there is a struggle with mental disorders, depression, and suicide. Having mental health issues is not something that is relegated to the secular world. In this short book, I propose that having true mental wellbeing is only had by application of biblical truth.

The apostle Paul states that as believers we have the mind of Christ.

Philippians 2:5-8 KJV
Let this mind be in you, which was also in Christ Jesus: [6] Who, being in the form of God, thought it not robbery to be equal with God: [7] But made himself of no reputation, and took upon him the form of a servant, and was made in the likeness of men:

[8] And being found in fashion as a man, he humbled himself, and became obedient unto death, even the death of the cross.

1 Corinthians 2:16 KJV
For who hath known the mind of the Lord, that he may instruct him? But we have the mind of Christ.

In Philippians chapter two, we see the mind of Christ is one of humility and service to others. It is a mind that is not focused only on your own needs, but the needs of others.

Philippians 2:4 KJV
Look not every man on his own things, but every man also on the things of others.

Part of good biblical mental health is tied to being a servant to others in helping them in their walk with the Lord in this broken world. By helping others we will help our own mental health.

In this book we will examine the following:

Chapter One: Made in the Image of God
Chapter Two: Having a Biblical Mindset
Chapter Three: The Battleground of the Mind
Chapter Four: Carnal Mind vs. Spiritual Mind
Chapter Five: Renewing Your Mind
Chapter Six: A Mind to Work

My goal in this work, in a direct and concise way, is to show you how to have a healthy biblical mindset to serve the Lord in this dark and perverse world.

Philippians 2:15-16 KJV
That ye may be blameless and harmless, the sons of God, without

rebuke, in the midst of a crooked and perverse nation, among whom ye shine as lights in the world; [16] Holding forth the word of life; that I may rejoice in the day of Christ, that I have not run in vain, neither laboured in vain.

CHAPTER ONE
MADE IN THE IMAGE OF GOD

Genesis 1:26 KJV

And God said, Let us make man in our image, after our likeness: and let them have dominion over the fish of the sea, and over the fowl of the air, and over the cattle, and over all the earth, and over every creeping thing that creepeth upon the earth.

From September of 1994 to March of 2002, my family and I lived in a smaller town outside of Toronto, Canada. Our purpose for moving to Canada was to minister the word of God. We lived in Halton Region in the town of Milton. One of the ways we were involved in the community was to be a volunteer within the Halton Regional Police Services. My wife and I worked in the Victim Services Unit where we helped victims of crime with the resources they needed to help them through their circumstances.

One time I went to court with a lady dealing with domestic violence issues. After court, in the parking lot, she communicated to me that she wished she could have a different life. I have also heard people say they wish there was a book on how to live your life. These kinds of statements come from those that do not have a relationship with Christ through his word.

The truth is there is a God, and he created us. He knows best how we are to live and have a fulfilling life bringing glory to him.

The reality is we do have a manual or book that shows us how to live in every aspect of our lives. It is called the Bible.

In order to have mental or spiritual health, we first need to understand how we are created by God.

Genesis 1:26-27 KJV
And God said, Let us make man in our image, after our likeness: and let them have dominion over the fish of the sea, and over the fowl of the air, and over the cattle, and over all the earth, and over every creeping thing that creepeth upon the earth. [27] So God created man in his own image, in the image of God created he him; male and female created he them.

God says, "Let us make man in our image." Who is the "us" and "our" referring to? This is the first indication of the Trinity in the Bible. God, or the Godhead, is one God with three functions as Father, Son, and Holy Spirit.

1 John 5:7 KJV
For there are three that bear record in heaven, the Father, the Word, and the Holy Ghost: and these three are one.

2 Corinthians 13:14 KJV
The grace of the Lord Jesus Christ, and the love of God, and the communion of the Holy Ghost, be with you all. Amen.

Just as creation reflects back to the Trinity, so does man. To be made in the image of God is to be that of a trinity ourselves. God made us with a spirit (mind), soul, and body. In the following verse, the apostle Paul is praying for the Thessalonians that they would be preserved blameless at the coming of our Lord Jesus Christ.

1 Thessalonians 5:23 KJV
And the very God of peace sanctify you wholly; and I pray God your whole spirit and soul and body be preserved blameless unto the coming of our Lord Jesus Christ.

Paul wanted the Thessalonians to be sanctified wholly or completely, which includes our spirit, soul, and body. Just as God is one God with three functions as Father, Son, and Spirit, we are one person with three different aspects. Our soul is the same as our spiritual heart. That is where our will is centered with our God-given ability to make our own choices. It's the soul where we have all our emotions.

Our body is our physical being, which is what all can see. We can't see our soul or spirit, but we can get some understanding of what's going on in our soul and spirit by our actions carried out in our body.

Now, let's talk about our spirit/mind, which is the subject of this book.

The Spirit of Your Mind

Ephesians 4:22-24 KJV
That ye put off concerning the former conversation the old man, which is corrupt according to the deceitful lusts; [23] And be renewed in the spirit of your mind; [24] And that ye put on the new man, which after God is created in righteousness and true holiness.

Verse 23 says, "and be renewed in the spirit of your mind." This is one verse that you see the connection of the spirit and mind. Grammatically, the source of our spirit is from our mind. This is why spiritual health is mental health. Interesting enough, when it comes to prayer, the Holy Spirit helps us to communicate our request to the Lord according to God's will. God the Father searches the mind of the Spirit to know exactly what our prayer request is. Again, you see that connection of mind and spirit.

Romans 8:27 KJV
And he that searcheth the hearts knoweth what is the mind of the Spirit, because he maketh intercession for the saints according to the will of God.

Back to Ephesians 4:23. Having a renewed mind appears between verse 22 and 24. I know that is a basic numerical truth, but my point is what those verses say. If we are to have a renewed mind, then we need to put off our former conversation and put on Christ.

Our former conversation is all about the lust and desires of the flesh. It is our lifestyle we had before we accepted Christ as our Lord and Savior. The word "conversation" is not just what we say; it is also what we do. We will have more to say about this in chapter five on renewing the mind. But for now let us finish this chapter by understanding that every action we take starts in the spirit of our mind.

Before we do anything, we have thought about it first. This thinking may be quick in a number of respects, but other decisions may take longer to think on before acting. Our thoughts will lead to the kind of attitude we will have. In turn our attitude will affect the kind of actions we have. Simply put, thoughts lead to attitudes, and attitudes lead to actions. If we have bad thoughts, then we will have bad attitudes and actions. But if we have biblical thoughts, we will have biblical attitudes and actions.

Having biblical and healthy thoughts will help us to be mentally/spiritually healthy. As Christians we have to feed our minds with the knowledge of God's word. The knowledge of the word is what will give us a biblical thought life. The only other option is the thoughts and philosophy of the world that will not help our mental stability. In the book of Proverbs, we see the need to have God's knowledge, understanding, and wisdom. You see these three words over and over again.

Proverbs 2:1-6 KJV
My son, if thou wilt receive my words, and hide my command-ments with thee; [2] So that thou incline thine ear unto wisdom, and apply thine heart to understanding; [3] Yea, if thou criest after knowledge, and liftest up thy voice for understanding; [4] If thou seekest her as silver, and searchest for her as for hid treasures; [5] Then shalt thou understand the fear of the LORD, and find the knowledge of God. [6] For the LORD giveth wisdom: out of his mouth cometh knowledge and understanding.

The source of true wisdom, understanding, and knowledge is from God's word. Wisdom is the word of God you understand and put into action (our body). Understanding what to do and choosing to do it comes from our will or heart (our soul). But as I said earlier, before we choose to do anything and act on that choice, we think about it first. Having knowledge of what to do deals with the thoughts we put into our mind/spirit.

In the above passage, we are exhorted or encouraged to cry after knowledge, understanding, and wisdom. In other words we need to ask God in prayer. This should be something that we do every time we read and study his word. We need to search for his knowledge like hidden treasure. If you knew you had treasure buried on your property or hidden somewhere in your home, you know you would search for it. That is the same attitude we need to have when it comes to searching out the word of God.

As we conclude this chapter on being made in the image of God, we need to understand the importance of that it is God that made us spirit, soul, and body. If we are to have a healthy mental condition throughout our life, then we need to seek and meditate on his word and not the thoughts and philosophy of the world. Your thought life should daily be filled with the word of God.

Psalm 1:1-2 KJV
Blessed is the man that walketh not in the counsel of the ungodly, nor standeth in the way of sinners, nor sitteth in the seat of the scornful. [2] But his delight is in the law of the LORD; and in his law doth he meditate day and night.

Colossians 1:9-10 KJV
For this cause we also, since the day we heard it, do not cease to pray for you, and to desire that ye might be filled with the knowledge of his will in all wisdom and spiritual understanding; [10] That ye might walk worthy of the Lord unto all pleasing, being fruitful in every good work, and increasing in the knowledge of God;

The word of God gives us the needed knowledge, understanding, and wisdom to feed the spirit of our mind so we can be in good mental and emotional health (our soul/heart) and have a walk that pleases the Lord.

CHAPTER TWO
HAVING A BIBLICAL MINDSET

2 Timothy 1:7 KJV
For God hath not given us the spirit of fear; but of power, and of love, and of a sound mind.

What Is Given to Us

After seeing that we are made in the image of God (with a spirit, soul, and body), now we need to gain a better understanding of the mind we have been given in Christ. The Lord has literally given us his mind through his word. We have the ability to read God's mind any time of the day or night. And what we need to do is let the mind of Christ to be in us. That only happens as we read and study the word.

Philippians 2:5 KJV
Let this mind be in you, which was also in Christ Jesus:

1 Corinthians 2:16 KJV
For who hath known the mind of the Lord, that he may instruct him? But we have the mind of Christ.

A lot of the time, the problem we have is neglecting the mind we have been given in Christ and we run our lives with our fleshly mind that desperately needs to be renewed (chapter five, "A Renewed Mind"). Remember, our own spirit is the same as our mind.

Ephesians 4:23 KJV
And be renewed in the spirit of your mind;

So, let's examine 2 Timothy 1:7 to see exactly the kind of spirit/mind we have been given.

A Spirit of Fear

This verse starts out with a clear understanding that we have NOT been given a spirit of fear.

Romans 8:15 KJV
For ye have not received the spirit of bondage again to fear; but ye have received the Spirit of adoption, whereby we cry, Abba, Father.

When we talk about fear in the Bible, there are two aspects. There is first the fear that we need to have, which is reverence and respect for God and his word (2 Corinthians 7:1). It is this fear that gives us the understanding we will be held accountable to God for our actions (2 Corinthians 5:10). But the fear that we are not supposed to have is the fear that causes bondage. To be bound is to be restricted from movement. There are people that, unfortunately, struggle with various phobias. Here are some of the most common phobias:

Achluophobia – "fear of darkness"
Acrophobia – "fear of heights"
Aerophobia – "fear of flying"

Claustrophobia – "fear of confined spaces"
Aquaphobia – "fear of water"
Enochlophobia – "fear of crowds"
Glossophobia – "fear of public speaking"
Hemophobia – "fear of blood"
Arachnophobia – "an irrational "fear of spiders"

Many of us may never have any kind of fear like the ones mentioned above. But we may have other circumstances that we do fear, and it restricts our walk and service to the Lord. As believers we have not received a spirit of fear to place us in any kind of bondage. If we find ourselves in fear of bondage, it is because we are not living in the mind/spirit we have been given in Christ.

One phobia I do want to reference is glossophobia, the fear of public speaking. I dare say there are a number of people that have this kind of fear. This is a fear that believers in Christ need to overcome. The Lord wants all of us to speak his word to others. That is how people are saved and come to the knowledge of the truth (Romans 10:9-15). If we are in fear to speak the word of God, then we are in bondage. We are allowing this fear to restrict us from the God-given job we have all been given. The apostle Paul commends those who grew in confidence to speak the word without fear, even though Paul was in prison for preaching the word.

If you have a fear of speaking the word, then you need to realize we have not been given a spirit of fear, but one of power that gives us the strength to fulfill God's will in our lives.

Philippians 1:14 KJV
And many of the brethren in the Lord, waxing confident by my bonds, are much more bold to speak the word without fear.

A Spirit of Power

2 Corinthians 4:6-7 KJV

For God, who commanded the light to shine out of darkness, hath shined in our hearts, to give the light of the knowledge of the glory of God in the face of Jesus Christ. [7] But we have this treasure in earthen vessels, that the excellency of the power may be of God, and not of us.

In Genesis chapter one, God said, "Let there be light." Due to Satan's rebellion, there is a darkness throughout the universe. But that darkness will not ever overcome the light. As believers in Christ, we have the light of the Lord Jesus Christ. Jesus, in his earthly ministry, said that he is the light of the world (John 8:12). In the above verse, Paul lays out how we have this same light in the knowledge of the glory of God in the face of Jesus Christ. It is no accident we see the word "knowledge" again. Remember, it is the knowledge of the word of God that we need to feed our own spirit or mind. That knowledge of Christ is also the source of our power.

Indeed, we are nothing but earthen vessels. No matter who we are, we are weak in our flesh. But through Jesus Christ, we have the power to accomplish all that the Lord would have us do. This is part of the biblical mindset we need to have. There is no way we can do the work that we are ordained to do (Ephesians 2:10) without having the proper mindset. We obtain this mindset by first understanding what we have been given in Christ.

We also need to understand anything that we do for the Lord that is worthy of his glory is only due to his power and not anything of us or our flesh. Again, the excellency of the power needs to be of God and not of us.

When it comes to serving the Lord, it is every believer's responsibility to do so. The work of the ministry is not just for the pastor or the deacon to do (Ephesians 4:12-16). Many do not serve the Lord because they think they don't know enough or they view themselves to not be capable or worthy to be used of God. This kind of thinking is the wrong mindset! Yes, we need to read, study, and apply the word of God in our lives. But to minister his word effectively, that does not depend on our meager strength but his power that we as believers have in us through Christ and the Spirit of God. The great apostle Paul never depended on his strength, but to the contrary, he ministered in the power and strength of the Lord. That is the biblical mindset we all need to have.

1 Thessalonians 1:5 KJV
For our gospel came not unto you in word only, but also in power, and in the Holy Ghost, and in much assurance; as ye know what manner of men we were among you for your sake.

Ephesians 3:20 KJV
Now unto him that is able to do exceeding abundantly above all that we ask or think, according to the power that worketh in us,

2 Corinthians 12:9 KJV
And he said unto me, My grace is sufficient for thee: for my strength is made perfect in weakness. Most gladly therefore will I rather glory in my infirmities, that the power of Christ may rest upon me.

A Spirit of Love
1 Corinthians 13:13 KJV
And now abideth faith, hope, charity, these three; but the greatest of these is charity.

No matter the dispensation or age throughout the word of

God man lives in, charity or love is the priority. God told the nation of Israel the following:

Deuteronomy 6:5 KJV
And thou shalt love the LORD thy God with all thine heart, and with all thy soul, and with all thy might.

When Jesus was asked what is the greatest commandment, he answered as follows:

Matthew 22:37-39 KJV
Jesus said unto him, Thou shalt love the Lord thy God with all thy heart, and with all thy soul, and with all thy mind. [38] This is the first and great commandment. [39] And the second is like unto it, Thou shalt love thy neighbour as thyself.

So, it is no surprise that love or charity is the priority in our dispensation of grace. We should love the Lord by doing the commandments he has given us through the apostle Paul. Paul writes to the church in Colosse that as they put off the old man and put on the new, they were to above all put on charity, which is the bond of perfectness.

Colossians 3:14 KJV
And above all these things put on charity, which is the bond of perfectness.

1 Timothy 1:5 KJV
Now the end of the commandment is charity out of a pure heart, and of a good conscience, and of faith unfeigned:

So as we talk about having a biblical mindset to serve the

Lord, we need to utilize this spirit/mind of love. Biblical charity is love in action. It is speaking the truth in love to others to help edify or build them up in their walk with the Lord (Ephesians 4:15-16).

Yes, I know what you are thinking. There are some hard people to love. Sometimes I joke with people that yes, I am commanded to love you, but the Bible says nothing about having to like you. In all seriousness we are to love others, and it can be hard to follow this commandment with some. But the capacity to biblically love others is not really within us. The source is from the Lord. That is why he has given us a spirit of love. Love is also part of the nine fruit of the Spirit that we have been sealed with the day we accepted Christ.

Galatians 5:22-23 KJV
But the fruit of the Spirit is love, joy, peace, longsuffering, gentleness, goodness, faith, [23] Meekness, temperance: against such there is no law.

It's by utilizing the fruit of the Spirit, which love is the first quality mentioned, is how we love others in order to serve them. Again, having a biblical mindset is about ministering the word of God and a relationship with Christ to others. That is why we are commanded to walk in love as Christ loved us. Understanding and applying the spirit of love is how we have the ability to do just that.

Ephesians 5:2 KJV
And walk in love, as Christ also hath loved us, and hath given himself for us an offering and a sacrifice to God for a sweetsmelling savour.

A Spirit of a Sound Mind

Even though we are talking about the mind, this aspect of the spirit that we have been given in Christ gets down to the heart of the matter. We have not been given a spirit or mind of fear, but of power, love, and a sound mind. We cannot have a biblical mindset without a sound mind.

We have all heard of a person's final will and testament starting off with the phrase, "Being of sound mind and body." What does it mean to be of a sound mind? In the world's definition, it is to have the mental capacity to understand the actions you are taking. Biblically speaking having a sound mind is a mind that is disciplined or in control. We can see the same thing in the biblical phrase of being sober minded.

Titus 2:6 KJV
Young men likewise exhort to be sober minded.

When we think of being sober, we typically only think in terms of not being drunk. Being sober minded is to not have anything controlling your mind or actions. Operating your life based on emotional instability is obviously not good. The Lord wants us to have a sober and sound mind. So how do we practically obtain a sound mind? The answer is filling our mind with sound words and sound doctrine.

2 Timothy 1:13 KJV
Hold fast the form of sound words, which thou hast heard of me, in faith and love which is in Christ Jesus.

Titus 1:9 KJV
Holding fast the faithful word as he hath been taught, that he

may be able by sound doctrine both to exhort and to convince the gainsayers.

In the above verses, we have to hold onto sound words and sound doctrine. Now, all of the word of God is sound words to learn from. When it comes to sound doctrine for us in the body of Christ in the dispensation of grace, it is the books written to us by the apostle of the Gentiles, Paul (Romans 11:13). That would be the books of Romans to Philemon. Daily reading and studying the word of God is how we obtain the spirit of a sound mind. The Lord has given us everything that we need to be of a sound mind. It is our job to hold fast to his sound words.

Before we conclude this chapter, we need to see why we need to have a spirit of power, love, and a sound mind.

Why It Was Given

As I say often, the Lord saved us not to sit but to serve him. If we are to serve him, then we need to have a biblical mindset to do so. We gain that mindset by operating in the spirit of power, love, and a sound mind.

Serving the Lord is the most rewarding and fulfilling time you will ever have on this planet. But biblically serving comes with suffering and tribulations as well. If you are not armed with a biblical mindset, then likely you will give up on serving and living for the Lord, and that is exactly what the enemy wants. The Lord will give you the power to overcome the afflictions, but you need to make sure you feed the spirit of your mind with his word so you can be of sound mind serving the Lord.

2 Ti.1:8-9 KJV
Be not thou therefore ashamed of the testimony of our Lord, nor

of me his prisoner: but be thou partaker of the afflictions of the gospel according to the power of God;

[9] Who hath saved us, and called us with an holy calling, not according to our works, but according to his own purpose and grace, which was given us in Christ Jesus before the world began,

CHAPTER THREE
THE BATTLEGROUND OF THE MIND

A Mind Corrupted

2 Corinthians 11:3 KJV But I fear, lest by any means, as the serpent beguiled Eve through his subtilty, so your minds should be corrupted from the simplicity that is in Christ.

After seeing the importance of how to have a biblical mind-set in order to minister, you can bet there will be an effort by Satan and this world to corrupt your mind. A corrupted mind is an unhealthy mind. An unhealthy mind is one that is not ready to serve the Lord. Without a doubt the battles we flight on a daily basis begin in the mind.

In the above verse, Paul had a great concern for the church at Corinth. There is simplicity in Christ, but Satan likes to complicate things by corrupting the word of God. You see that from the very beginning as Paul gives the example of Satan with Eve. The first question ever asked in the Bible was by the serpent/ Satan questioning what God said. When you allow doubt about the word of God to creep into your mind, you are on the path to have your mind corrupted. This is the same tactic Satan continues to this day.

Genesis 3:1 KJV

Now the serpent was more subtil than any beast of the field which the LORD God had made. And he said unto the woman, Yea, hath God said, Ye shall not eat of every tree of the garden?

Not only does Satan question the word of God, he also wants to exalt himself above God and his word. When God created Lucifer, he gave him a position on earth in the Garden of Eden with his own throne. But that was not good enough for Lucifer, and he attempted to exalt his throne above the stars of God and became Satan, which means adversary (Isaiah 14:12-15, Eze. 28:13-16). Satan's sin is largely looked at as pride. He lifted himself up against God and his will. And, just like Satan, man with a corrupt mind will have the same rebellious actions. We see an example of this with man not too long after the flood in Genesis chapter eleven.

Genesis 11:1-6 KJV
And the whole earth was of one language, and of one speech. [2] And it came to pass, as they journeyed from the east, that they found a plain in the land of Shinar; and they dwelt there. [3] And they said one to another, Go to, let us make brick, and burn them throughly. And they had brick for stone, and slime had they for morter. [4] And they said, Go to, let us build us a city and a tower, whose top may reach unto heaven; and let us make us a name, lest we be scattered abroad upon the face of the whole earth. [5] And the LORD came down to see the city and the tower, which the children of men builded. [6] And the LORD said, Behold, the people is one, and they have all one language; and this they begin to do: and now nothing will be restrained from them, which they have imagined to do.

It was God's plan, even after the flood, for man to populate the earth just like he commanded Adam and Eve (Genesis 1:26-

28). But instead of obeying God's word, the world comes together as one to build a city with a tower whose top could reach into heaven lest they be spread abroad over the face of the earth. This tower was more than just building a skyscraper. But that is the subject of another book. Bottom line man was going against what the Lord intended for him in his word.

Before we move on from this passage, there is something of note that needs to be brought to light. God makes a stunning statement about man at this time and is the reason why he confounds the languages.

Genesis 11:6 KJV
And the LORD said, Behold, the people is one, and they have all one language; and this they begin to do: and now nothing will be restrained from them, which they have imagined to do.

This statement from the Lord lets us know there was more going on than man building a city with a tall building. They had every intent to go off of Planet Earth and into heaven. That is the same thing we have seen with man in our modern era. The Lord said that man in his current condition would be able to do anything they imagined to do. It is that word "imagine" or "imagination" that demands our attention. This word is never used in a good context in scripture. It is always against God and his word. Just as we have seen with the tower of Babel, we see the same today.

Romans 1:21 KJV
Because that, when they knew God, they glorified him not as God, neither were thankful; but became vain in their imaginations, and their foolish heart was darkened.

In Romans chapter one, verses 21 through 32, we see the downfall of man in his sinful nature. We are prone to all kinds of sin. The reason this happened is because when we knew God, we glorified him not as God and neither were we thankful. What was the result? Man became vain or empty in his imaginations. Remember, our imaginations deal with our thoughts. Our thoughts are centered on our spirit or mind. Having vain imaginations in our mind leads to darkness on our soul or heart. The end result of that is sinful actions.

The apostle Paul warns us to not walk as the other Gentiles walk in the vanity of their mind. A Gentile is any person that is not of Jewish descent. The church or body of Christ is largely made up of Gentiles, but once we are in Christ, we are no longer looked on by God as Gentiles. Now that our position is in Christ, we are to walk accordingly. Our walk should not be in the vain mind of Gentiles that leads to all kinds of sinful actions. But our walk should be according to the renewed mind we have in Christ.

Ephesians 4:17-19 KJV
This I say therefore, and testify in the Lord, that ye henceforth walk not as other Gentiles walk, in the vanity of their mind, [18] Having the understanding darkened, being alienated from the life of God through the ignorance that is in them, because of the blindness of their heart: [19] Who being past feeling have given themselves over unto lasciviousness, to work all uncleanness with greediness.

A Mind Defended

So, how do we protect ourselves from having a corrupted mind? The answer goes beyond just saying I need to read the word of God. Daily, we are faced with all kinds of thoughts and world philosophies that are against the word of God. The sources of these vain imaginations reach us through various means. There is television, newspapers, and magazines, as well as social media through our smart phones. We also engage family, friends, and coworkers who do not operate their lives on biblical truth. We also even fight our own thoughts and feelings we had before we were in Christ. This is why it is necessary we renew our mind through the mind of Christ.

After recognizing the sources of vain imaginations or corrupted thoughts, we need to fight to get rid of them so they don't affect our mind or thinking. Remember, thoughts lead to attitudes that lead to actions. I want to share an Old Testament story that illustrates this spiritual truth for us today.

Asa was king of Judah when the nation of Israel was split into two kingdoms. This happened after Solomon was king. The northern 10 tribes were ruled by kings that came from the line of Jeroboam. Judah and Benjamin were ruled through the descendants of Solomon. All of Israel had problems worshipping false gods of the nations around them. A majority of kings in the northern kingdom and some in the southern kingdom allowed this false worship to continue. But that was not the case with Asa.

2 Chronicles 14:2-4 KJV
And Asa did that which was good and right in the eyes of the LORD his God: [3] For he took away the altars of the strange gods, and the high places, and brake down the images, and cut down the groves: [4] And commanded Judah to seek the LORD God of their fathers, and to do the law and the commandment.

One of the things Asa did was to take away the high places. Israel had a huge problem of worshipping strange gods in the high places. The high places were areas on hills and mountains dedicated to these practices. It should be no surprise this false worship took place on hills and mountains. This ties right back to Satan and his rebelling against God. Satan tried to exalt his God-given throne above God himself so he would be worshipped (Isaiah 14:12-15). God stopped Satan and the third of the angels that sided with Satan and cast them down. That was the start of this spiritual war that is still raging today. As believers in Christ, we have to realize that we are very much a part of this warfare that begins in our mind.

Just as Asa tore down these high places of false worship, we need to cast down every high thing that exalts itself against Christ.

2 Corinthians 10:3-5 KJV
For though we walk in the flesh, we do not war after the flesh: [4] (For the weapons of our warfare are not carnal, but mighty through God to the pulling down of strong holds;) [5] Casting down imaginations, and every high thing that exalteth itself against the knowledge of God, and bringing into captivity every thought to the obedience of Christ;

We all are faced with strongholds, imaginations, and high things that exalt themselves against the knowledge of God. The above passage of scripture indicates that there will never be a time while living on this earth that we will not have these things. The issue is what do we do when we have these imaginations and high things that combat our mind? Do we meditate and dwell on them so they affect our attitudes and actions? Or do we pull down and cast down these thoughts and imaginations that are against Christ?

This is so vital in having mental health biblically. Every bad thought needs to be brought into captivity to Christ. We do this by the spiritual armor and weapon of the word of God that has been given to us to fight this battle.

Romans 13:11-12 KJV
And that, knowing the time, that now it is high time to awake out of sleep: for now is our salvation nearer than when we believed. [12] The night is far spent, the day is at hand: let us therefore cast off the works of darkness, and let us put on the armour of light.

Ephesians 6:10-18 KJV
Finally, my brethren, be strong in the Lord, and in the power of his might. [11] Put on the whole armour of God, that ye may be able to stand against the wiles of the devil. [12] For we wrestle not against flesh and blood, but against principalities, against powers, against the rulers of the darkness of this world, against spiritual wickedness in high places. [13] Wherefore take unto you the whole armour of God, that ye may be able to withstand in the evil day, and having done all, to stand. [14] Stand therefore, having your loins girt about with truth, and having on the breastplate of righteousness; [15] And your feet shod with the preparation of the gospel of peace; [16] Above all, taking the shield of faith, wherewith ye shall be able to quench all the fiery darts of the wicked. [17] And take the helmet of salvation, and the sword of the Spirit, which is the word of God: [18] Praying always with all prayer and supplication in the Spirit, and watching thereunto with all perseverance and supplication for all saints;

The book of Ephesians is known for being the book on spiritual warfare. That is why chapter six lays out the seven pieces of the armor of God we need to dress ourselves with daily. First and foremost we have to understand our battle is not with flesh and blood. Our battle is with Satan and his cohorts. It is interesting to note that they are described as spiritual wickedness in "high places."

Each piece of the armor is vital, but there are three I want to highlight to help us defend against having a corrupted mind. Above all we are to take up the shield of faith. We need to have on the helmet of salvation and in our other hand the sword of the Spirit. The shield, the helmet, and the sword can all be defined by the word of God. As a matter of fact, every piece of the armor of God relates back to the word of God.

Satan, or the Wicked, is going to shoot fiery darts at us that we can quench by the shield of faith. We grow in our faith by hearing the word of God (Romans 10:17).

The helmet of salvation protects our head. That directly relates to our mind and thoughts. Too many Christians struggle with whether they are saved or not because they buy into Satan's questioning the word of God (Genesis 3:1). In the same book of Ephesians, we are sealed with the Holy Spirit of God once we believe in Christ (Ephesians 1:12-13). In other words, we cannot lose our salvation since we are sealed until the day of redemption.

Finally, the Lord gives us the sword of the Spirit, which is the word of God. It is this sword that we need to grow in our confidence to use to cut down every immigration and high thought that is against the truth of the word. The word of God is quick (defined as living) and powerful. It is able to discern between our soul and spirit, as well as the joints and marrow, which is our body. It is no accident that in the following verse that lays this truth out deals with all three aspects of man: spirit, soul, and body.

Hebrews 4:12 KJV
For the word of God is quick, and powerful, and sharper than

any twoedged sword, piercing even to the dividing asunder of soul and spirit, and of the joints and marrow, and is a discerner of the thoughts and intents of the heart.

So when Satan whispers in your ears that God can't use you because of all the sins you have done, you respond with God's word.

Romans 5:20 KJV
Moreover the law entered, that the offence might abound. But where sin abounded, grace did much more abound:

When Satan tells you are all alone and no one cares for you, you respond with God's word.

2 Timothy 4:17 KJV
Notwithstanding the Lord stood with me, and strengthened me; that by me the preaching might be fully known, and that all the Gentiles might hear: and I was delivered out of the mouth of the lion.

When you are going through physical difficulties or sickness and Satan uses that to make you depressed, you respond with the word of God.

2 Corinthians 12:9-10 KJV
And he said unto me, My grace is sufficient for thee: for my strength is made perfect in weakness. Most gladly therefore will I rather glory in my infirmities, that the power of Christ may rest upon me. [10] Therefore I take pleasure in infirmities, in reproaches, in necessities, in persecutions, in distresses for Christ's sake: for when I am weak, then am I strong.

It is my hope that you see the point I am making in how to practically defend yourself with the word of God against the attacks of the enemy. Whether the attack is coming from Satan, the world, or your own flesh, staying mentally healthy depends on you using the weapon of the word of God given to us as a believer in Christ.

CHAPTER FOUR
CARNAL MIND VS. SPIRITUAL MIND

Romans 8:5-8 KJV
For they that are after the flesh do mind the things of the flesh; but they that are after the Spirit the things of the Spirit. [6] For to be carnally minded is death; but to be spiritually minded is life and peace. [7] Because the carnal mind is enmity against God: for it is not subject to the law of God, neither indeed can be. [8] So then they that are in the flesh cannot please God.

To be carnal is to do those things that please our flesh/body. A great example of this is going to a carnival. All of the lights, rides, games, activities, and food are designed to please your flesh. Of course, our flesh is never satisfied.

Ecclesiastes 1:8 KJV
All things are full of labour; man cannot utter it: the eye is not satisfied with seeing, nor the ear filled with hearing.

The first verse of the above passage says the following:
For they that are after the flesh do mind the things of the flesh, but they that are after the Spirit the things of the Spirit.
Here we see the body and mind connection. Our body can and most likely will act out what we put into our mind. If we

mind the things of the flesh, then fleshly actions will be manifested. The same is true spiritually. We need to be spiritually minded through application of the word of God in order to have spiritual or biblical actions.

In verse six we see the results of being carnal minded and spiritually minded. The carnal mind leads to death. There is nothing good that comes from being carnally minded. But to be spiritually minded leads to life and peace.

For to be carnally minded is death, but to be spiritually minded is life and peace.

I believe that everyone wants a great life and peace of heart and mind. How we obtain that is something that may be of debate. Some think a great life and peace will come from having a high-paying job, fame, and other social economic advantages. Having these things will never guarantee lasting peace. That kind of thinking comes from a carnal mind.

When we live our lives by the thinking of a carnal mind and it fails to satisfy, then depression can set in. We can start to have self-esteem and other mental health issues. If we do not tap into the source of peace that we have as believers in Christ, we can look to more carnal sources to try and have some measure of peace. That may include excessive drinking, drugs, and other addictive behaviors. These things may provide temporary relief but will ultimately leave you worse off. Thus, people get locked into a downward spiral that is hard to come back from, but not impossible. Indeed, with God all things are possible.

Mark 10:27 KJV
And Jesus looking upon them saith, With men it is impossible, but not with God: for with God all things are possible.

To have life and peace, we need to change our thinking from

the carnal mind. The carnal mind only wants to please the flesh or ourselves. To have true lasting peace will come from walking in the Spirit by walking in the word of God. To be spiritually minded is to serve the Lord by serving others. We will never be fulfilled in our lives unless we are doing what the Lord has called us to do. To be spiritually minded is really not a hard or mystical concept. The word of God is a living spiritual book (Hebrews 4:12). As I spend time reading the word of God, I am putting spiritual thoughts into my natural or carnal mind. I cleanse my carnal mind by washing it with the water of the word of God.

Ephesians 5:26-27 KJV
That he might sanctify and cleanse it with the washing of water by the word, [27] That he might present it to himself a glorious church, not having spot, or wrinkle, or any such thing; but that it should be holy and without blemish.

The last two verses I need to cover from Romans 8:5-8 deal with the enmity that is between the carnal mind and God.

[7] Because the carnal mind is enmity against God: for it is not subject to the law of God, neither indeed can be. [8] So then they that are in the flesh cannot please God.

To have enmity against God is to have hatred. The word enmity is closely related to the word enemy. This makes the gravity of having a carnal mind of upmost seriousness. Simply put the Lord hates a carnal mind, and there is no way we can do those things that please him with carnal thinking carried out by our actions in the flesh. It is our actions that determine whether we are pleasing God or not.

Another way to think about this is laid out in the book of

Galatians. In chapter five we have a detailed look at what it is to walk in the Spirit of God or to walk in our flesh. There are no in-between or gray areas. We are either walking in the flesh or Spirit. We are either being carnally minded or spiritually minded. We are either doing the things that please God or not.

Galatians 5:16-23 KJV

This I say then, Walk in the Spirit, and ye shall not fulfil the lust of the flesh. [17] For the flesh lusteth against the Spirit, and the Spirit against the flesh: and these are contrary the one to the other: so that ye cannot do the things that ye would. [18] But if ye be led of the Spirit, ye are not under the law. [19] Now the works of the flesh are manifest, which are these; Adultery, fornication, uncleanness, lasciviousness, [20] Idolatry, witchcraft, hatred, variance, emulations, wrath, strife, seditions, heresies, [21] Envyings, murders, drunkenness, revellings, and such like: of the which I tell you before, as I have also told you in time past, that they which do such things shall not inherit the kingdom of God. [22] But the fruit of the Spirit is love, joy, peace, longsuffering, gentleness, goodness, faith, [23] Meekness, temperance: against such there is no law.

In the above passage, there are 17 specific works of the flesh and 9 fruit of the Spirit. Since we are born with a sinful nature, due to Adam's sin (Romans 5:12), we naturally are prone to these works of the flesh. Being born again through Jesus Christ, we also are sealed with the Holy Spirit and have these nine qualities of the fruit of the Spirit:

love, joy, peace, longsuffering, gentleness, goodness, faith, meekness, and temperance.

It is these aspects of the Spirit that we need to use daily in our lives. That happens as we learn from the word how we are to love. The Bible shows us the source of joy we have in Christ. The word gives us plenty of examples of circumstances that require long suffering. Each and every part of the fruit of the Spirit is grown in us as we feed our mind and heart the word of God.

In the next chapter, we will detail the biblical process of renewing our mind. But I wanted to end this chapter on the carnal mind vs. the spiritual mind with the following passage:

Philippians 4:6-9 KJV
Be careful for nothing; but in every thing by prayer and supplication with thanksgiving let your requests be made known unto God. [7] And the peace of God, which passeth all understanding, shall keep your hearts and minds through Christ Jesus. [8] Finally, brethren, whatsoever things are true, whatsoever things are honest, whatsoever things are just, whatsoever things are pure, whatsoever things are lovely, whatsoever things are of good report; if there be any virtue, and if there be any praise, think on these things. [9] Those things, which ye have both learned, and received, and heard, and seen in me, do: and the God of peace shall be with you.

There are three things to consider in this passage in order to have peace through being spiritually minded.

Prayer

In verse six we need to be careful for nothing. In other words we should not be full of care and concern. That is why we are commanded to pray. We need to let the Lord know the things that are on our heart. As we make our requests known to the Lord, we cannot forget to be thankful for the things he had done for us. This is something that should be a lifestyle for us. We should have a consistent and continual prayer life (1 Thessalonians 5:16-18).

The result of praying will be obtaining peace of God in our

hearts and minds. You will note that verse seven does not say the Lord will answer all of your requests. We know the Lord answers prayers. The answer may be yes, no, or not yet. But what we really need is peace of heart and mind. Again, the heart is dealing with our soul and emotions, and the mind or spirit deals with our thoughts. Going to the Lord in prayer is key to being mentally healthy. Praying God's word helps us to be spiritually minded in order to have life and peace.

Pondering

The next verse lays out the right things we need to ponder or think about so we can be spiritually minded. In Philippians 4:8 the Lord gives us eight things we need to think on instead of carnal thoughts. The number eight in the Bible is the number of new beginnings. One classic example is Noah's flood. It was only Noah's family that got on the ark, which were eight people. It is by them that we have our population on earth today. The Lord started over again with eight people. Even in our everyday world we see this truth as we are driving in residential neighborhoods. When you come to a stop sign, you are supposed to stop, look for traffic, and then begin again. It is interesting that the shape of a stop sign is an octagon, which has eight sides.

So, if we want to be spiritually minded, we need to think on these eight things instead of the things of the world and our carnal mind. This is something that we will see in some detail in chapter five on renewing your mind.

Practice

Finally, if we are to have the peace of God in our lives, then we should not only pray and ponder the word. To have the peace of God, we also need to do what the word of God commands us to do. Paul says in verse nine to do those things that we have learned, seen, and heard of him. Those things are laid out for us in the books that he writes to us from Romans through Philemon. The Lord used Paul to communicate doctrine to the church, the body of Christ. All of the Bible is for us, but not all of the Bible is to us. This is important to understand so that we are not taking God's word out of context and trying to keep a doctrine that the Lord has not intended for us.

If we want the God of peace to be with us in a daily, practical way, then we need to apply his word to our lives. It is not enough to just know the word of God and even understand it. We need to daily put it into practice. To be spiritually minded as opposed to being carnally minded does not happen automatically. It takes effort on our part. The Lord has given us everything we need to do so. But we have to be diligent in spending time daily in the word of God.

CHAPTER FIVE
A RENEWED MIND

Romans 12:2 KJV
And be not conformed to this world: but be ye transformed by the renewing of your mind, that ye may prove what is that good, and acceptable, and perfect, will of God.

Now, it's time to get down to the heart of the matter. We have seen that the battle takes place in the mind in chapter three. Chapter four shows us the results of being carnally minded verses spiritual minded. If we are going to be spiritually minded, then we need to renew our mind daily with the mind of Christ, which is his word.

One of the references that we covered in the previous chapter on the carnal mind vs. the spiritual mind is the following:

Galatians 5:16-17KJV
This I say then, Walk in the Spirit, and ye shall not fulfil the lust of the flesh. [17] For the flesh lusteth against the Spirit, and the Spirit against the flesh: and these are contrary the one to the other: so that ye cannot do the things that ye would.

The battle of walking in the Spirit so we don't fulfill the lusts of the flesh is a constant one. Daily, we feel the pull of our flesh, the world, and even temptations thrown at us from Satan. That is why it is imperative we daily renew our mind.

We all go through circumstances that mentally wear on us. These things can weigh us down and, if not biblically dealt with, can lead to depression and looking for peace in all the wrong places. Even the mighty warrior and the second king of Israel, David, dealt with mental stress and even despair.

1 Samuel 21:10-15 KJV

And David arose, and fled that day for fear of Saul, and went to Achish the king of Gath. [11] And the servants of Achish said unto him, Is not this David the king of the land? Did they not sing one to another of him in dances, saying, Saul hath slain his thousands, and David his ten thousands? [12] And David laid up these words in his heart, and was sore afraid of Achish the king of Gath. [13] And he changed his behaviour before them, and feigned himself mad in their hands, and scrabbled on the doors of the gate, and let his spittle fall down upon his beard. [14] Then said Achish unto his servants, Lo, ye see the man is mad: wherefore then have ye brought him to me? [15] Have I need of mad men, that ye have brought this fellow to play the mad man in my presence? shall this fellow come into my house?

David was on the run from King Saul, who was trying to kill him. He escapes to the land of the Philistines where Achish is king in Gath. David fakes being a mad man (crazy) to avoid capture or suspicion since he was a well-known warrior for Israel. Then he escapes to take refuge in a cave. That had to be a very low point for David in his life. Probably even more so when he knows he had been anointed to be the next king of Israel.

If that was not enough, he then has 400 people who came to him in the cave that all had their own problems. The last thing

David needed was 400 problem people that you would think would not help his situation at all but make it worse.

1 Samuel 22:1-2 KJV
David therefore departed thence, and escaped to the cave Adullam: and when his brethren and all his father's house heard it, they went down thither to him. [2] And every one that was in distress, and every one that was in debt, and every one that was discontented, gathered themselves unto him; and he became a captain over them: and there were with him about four hundred men.

Instead of David saying, "Get out of here and find your own cave," he does something that most of us probably would not think to do. David becomes a captain over them. He becomes a leader to them and an example of trusting and following the Lord. It is out of these 400 that become David's mighty men in battle. They went from being depressed, in debt, and discontented to being used of the Lord.

2 Samuel 23:8-10 KJV
These be the names of the mighty men whom David had: The Tachmonite that sat in the seat, chief among the captains; the same was Adino the Eznite: he lift up his spear against eight hundred, whom he slew at one time. [9] And after him was Eleazar the son of Dodo the Ahohite, one of the three mighty men with David, when they defied the Philistines that were there gathered together to battle, and the men of Israel were gone away: [10] He arose, and smote the Philistines until his hand was weary, and his hand clave unto the sword: and the LORD wrought a great victory that day; and the people returned after him only to spoil.

In another incident even David's mighty men were so distraught over the enemy taking their wives and children and burning their city that they wanted to kill David. I want you to notice how David handled this situation remembering that David also had his family taken.

1 Samuel 30:1-6 KJV

And it came to pass, when David and his men were come to Ziklag on the third day, that the Amalekites had invaded the south, and Ziklag, and smitten Ziklag, and burned it with fire; [2] And had taken the women captives, that were therein: they slew not any, either great or small, but carried them away, and went on their way. [3] So David and his men came to the city, and, behold, it was burned with fire; and their wives, and their sons, and their daughters, were taken captives. [4] Then David and the people that were with him lifted up their voice and wept, until they had no more power to weep. [5] And David's two wives were taken captives, Ahinoam the Jezreelitess, and Abigail the wife of Nabal the Carmelite. [6] And David was greatly distressed; for the people spake of stoning him, because the soul of all the people was grieved, every man for his sons and for his daughters: but David encouraged himself in the Lord his God.

David encouraged himself in the Lord. There are a few observations we need to see from these two stories to implement in our lives.

In 1 Samuel chapter 22, David becomes a leader to these men. Instead of dwelling on his own problems, he led the 400 out of theirs and they became profitable for the Lord. Too often we get so focused on our own issues and forget to see the needs of others. By focusing only on our circumstances, we can make ourselves more depressed and stressed instead of giving it to the Lord and then ministering to others. God even gives us comfort in all we go through from his word so we can turn around and comfort others. Ministering to others will also help your mental health.

2 Corinthians 1:3-4 KJV
Blessed be God, even the Father of our Lord Jesus Christ, the Father of mercies, and the God of all comfort; [4] Who comforteth us in all our tribulation, that we may be able to comfort them which are in any trouble, by the comfort wherewith we ourselves are comforted of God.

Secondly, and perhaps most importantly, when all seemed lost for David and even his men were so mentally distraught at the taking of their families that they wanted to kill David, he did not forsake the Lord. To the contrary he encouraged himself in the Lord. If you find yourself feeling all alone even at this moment, as a believer in Christ, you are not. The Lord is always with you whether you feel like he is or not. He is there to encourage and strengthen you to make it through the most difficult of circumstances.

2 Timothy 4:16-18 KJV
At my first answer no man stood with me, but all men forsook me: I pray God that it may not be laid to their charge. [17] Notwithstanding the Lord stood with me, and strengthened me; that by me the preaching might be fully known, and that all the Gentiles might hear: and I was delivered out of the mouth of the lion. [18] And the Lord shall deliver me from every evil work, and will preserve me unto his heavenly kingdom: to whom be glory for ever and ever. Amen.

So, you might ask me, how do you renew your mind? How

do I stop thinking about the negative in a situation and focus on the positive or what's biblical? Glad you asked. If we are to be spiritually minded instead of being carnally minded, then we have to let the mind of Christ dwell in us. That happens as we spend time in the word of God. We need to read, study, meditate, and apply his word in order to change our mindset.

Remember, thoughts lead to attitudes, and attitudes lead to actions. If you are dwelling on bad thoughts, then don't be surprised about having a bad attitude. If your bad attitude doesn't change, then it will affect your actions.

That is why we need to change our mental focus to dwelling on biblical thoughts. The only way you get biblical thoughts is by spending the time in God's word. This is why the battleground is the mind and what we think about is such a key to having biblical mental health.

Sprit (Mind) – Thoughts – Knowledge

Soul (Heart/Will) – Attitude – Understanding

Body (Physical Being) – Actions – Wisdom

Let's review what Solomon says to his son.

Proverbs 2:1-6 KJV

My son, if thou wilt receive my words, and hide my commandments with thee; [2] So that thou incline thine ear unto wisdom, and apply thine heart to understanding; [3] Yea, if thou criest after knowledge, and liftest up thy voice for understanding; [4] If thou seekest her as silver, and searchest for her as for hid treasures; [5] Then shalt thou understand the fear of the Lord, and find the knowledge of God. [6] For the Lord giveth wisdom: out of his mouth cometh knowledge and understanding.

In the above passage, we need to seek God's word like we are on a treasure hunt. It is from the word of God that we gain the needed knowledge, understanding, and wisdom to be mentally/ spiritually healthy.

When we talk about renewing your mind, it is not a suggestion for the Christian. It is a command given to us by God. It is a command that needs to be obeyed. Having a renewed mind is to our benefit, and it is a benefit we need daily. Why is that? Because daily we are bombarded by the lusts of our own flesh, as well as the pull of the world against the things of God.

Renewing Your Mind

Let's examine the key verse in this chapter:

Romans 12:2 KJV
And be not conformed to this world: but be ye transformed by the renewing of your mind, that ye may prove what is that good, and acceptable, and perfect, will of God.

Again, this is a command that has three basic parts. First, we are not to be conformed to this world. Unfortunately we have too many churches and Christians that are doing just that. They are conforming their churches and themselves to the way the world works. We see this basic thought pervading the church today with making their services and messages more like a worldly entertainment event with a motivational speech by the pastor in order to attract more people and not potentially offend them with the word of God. They are literally doing what we are commanded not to do. The world is against God and the things of God.

John 15:18-19 KJV
If the world hate you, ye know that it hated me before it hated you. [19] If ye were of the world, the world would love his own: but

because ye are not of the world, but I have chosen you out of the world, therefore the world hateth you.

Galatians 6:14 KJV
But God forbid that I should glory, save in the cross of our Lord Jesus Christ, by whom the world is crucified unto me, and I unto the world.

The world's thinking is against God's word. That is why you see the apostle Paul state in the above verse he is crucified to the world and the world is crucified to him. In other words he is dead to the world and vice versa. The ways of the world have no effect on him, and the same needs to be true with us. It is easy to be conformed to the world since we are born into this world with a sinful nature. Once we are in Christ, we need to go through the process of being transformed from the thinking of the world to the truth of the word of God, or the mind of Christ.

The Replacement Principle

God never asks you to just stop doing bad behavior without replacing it with biblical action. Ephesians chapter four is a great example of this. Instead of lying we are to speak truth (Eph. 4:25). Instead of stealing we are to labor and be ready to give to others (Eph. 4:28). Instead of having corrupt communication, we are to have words that edify or build others up (Eph. 4:29). We are only able to do these things if we first replace our old conversation with the new conversation we have in Christ. The English word "conversation" goes beyond how we use the word today. Conversation in its true meaning deals with your manner of living. The word encompasses what you do and say.

In the following passage, we will examine our previous walk as Gentiles (non-Jewish people) and the walk or conversation we are to have in Christ.

Ephesians 4:17-24 KJV
This I say therefore, and testify in the Lord, that ye henceforth walk not as other Gentiles walk, in the vanity of their mind, [18] Having the understanding darkened, being alienated from the life of God through the ignorance that is in them, because of the blindness of their heart: [19] Who being past feeling have given themselves over unto lasciviousness, to work all uncleanness with greediness. [20] But ye have not so learned Christ; [21] If so be that ye have heard him, and have been taught by him, as the truth is in Jesus: [22] That ye put off concerning the former conversation the old man, which is corrupt according to the deceitful lusts; [23] And be re-newed in the spirit of your mind; [24] And that ye put on the new man, which after God is created in righteousness and true holiness.

There is a lot that Paul lays out describing how Gentiles walk in the vanity of their mind in contrast to how we are to walk with a renewed spirit of our mind in Christ. To have a vain mind is to have a mind void of anything that is pleasing to the Lord. Remember, thoughts lead to attitude, which leads to actions. Paul lays out the actions or results from a vain mind.

...have given themselves over unto lasciviousness, to work all uncleanness with greediness

That word "lasciviousness" means lewd sexual behavior. That is coupled with working all uncleanness and greediness. In other words a vain mind is a mind that is only focused on pleasing the flesh and not pleasing the Lord (chapter four of this book).

As believers in Christ, we are to put off the former conver-sation of our vain Gentile mind and be renewed in the spirit of our mind. Just because we are now in Christ doesn't mean we will automatically walk according to the word of God. As this passage says, we need to put off the former conversation and be renewed in the spirit of our mind by putting on Christ. The image is that of taking off old dirty clothes and putting on fresh clean clothes. Again, this is the Lord's replacement principle that we need to follow daily and throughout the day in order to have a renewed mind. If we fail to do this, then we can resort back to walking in a vain mind. The way that we put on Christ, have our mind renewed, is to daily spend time in the word of God and applying it to our lives.

2 Corinthians 4:16 KJV
For which cause we faint not; but though our outward man perish, yet the inward man is renewed day by day.

Peace of Mind

The result of having a renewed mind is to have a mind at peace. Ultimately we all want peace in our lives, but many go about trying to obtain peace in all the wrong ways. That comes from wrong thinking:

"If I land the right job…"

"If I make this much money…"

"If I was famous…"

"If I had a better home or car…"

And yet others try to drown out their problems and issues by drinking too much, doing drugs, or indulging in other addictive behaviors.

True lasting peace will only come through a relationship with Christ.

John 14:27 KJV

Peace I leave with you, my peace I give unto you: not as the world giveth, give I unto you. Let not your heart be troubled, neither let it be afraid.

John 16:33 KJV
These things I have spoken unto you, that in me ye might have peace. In the world ye shall have tribulation: but be of good cheer; I have overcome the world.

In order for us to have the peace OF God, we need to have peace WITH God first. We are born in sin with a sinful nature we inherited from Adam (Romans 5:12). That sin separates us from God, ultimately leading us to spend eternity in hell. But Jesus paid that debt for us (Romans 6:23). By placing our faith in the Lord Jesus Christ, we are declared just or righteous before God the Father and we have peace with God.

Romans 5:1 KJV
Therefore being justified by faith, we have peace with God through our Lord Jesus Christ:

And now that we have peace with God, we have access to the peace of God daily. The way we access this peace that passes all human understanding is by talking to the Lord about all the things that trouble us and by the application of his word. It really is that simple, but our problem is we don't take God at his word. In other words we don't believe his word will actually work for us. That's the wrong kind of thinking or thoughts.

1 Thessalonians 2:13 KJV
For this cause also thank we God without ceasing, because, when ye received the word of God which ye heard of us, ye received it not

as the word of men, but as it is in truth, the word of God, which effectually worketh also in you that believe.

The word of God will be effective in our lives if we believe it! To have a mind at peace is to have a renewed mind. We renew our mind by keeping it focused on Christ and his word.

Isaiah 26:3-4 KJV
Thou wilt keep him in perfect peace, whose mind is stayed on thee : because he trusteth in thee. [4] Trust ye in the Lord for ever: for in the Lord Jehovah is everlasting strength:

Philippians 4:6-9 KJV
Be careful for nothing; but in every thing by prayer and supplication with thanksgiving let your requests be made known unto God. [7] And the peace of God, which passeth all understanding, shall keep your hearts and minds through Christ Jesus. [8] Finally, brethren, whatsoever things are true, whatsoever things are honest, whatsoever things are just, whatsoever things are pure, whatsoever things are lovely, whatsoever things are of good report; if there be any virtue, and if there be any praise, think on these things. [9] Those things, which ye have both learned, and received, and heard, and seen in me, do: and the God of peace shall be with you.

CHAPTER SIX
A MIND TO WORK

Review of the Last Five Chapters

In chapter one we saw we are made in the image of God, which is the Trinity. We are spirit/mind, soul, and body (1 Thessalonians 5:23).

In chapter two we saw how we need to have a biblical mindset that ultimately is needed for serving the Lord. God has not given us a spirit of fear, but of power, love, and a sound mind (2 Timothy 1:7).

In chapter three we saw that the battleground is the mind. Daily we fight against imaginations and thoughts that are against God and his word. We need to cast down those things in order to have a mind that is focused on the Lord (2 Corinthians 10:5).

In chapter four we continue to examine the carnal mind vs. the spiritual mind. The final result of a carnal mind is death. But the end result of a spiritual mind is life and peace (Romans 8:5-8).

In chapter five we saw that renewing your mind really is the nuts and bolts of being mentally healthy biblically. We saw the importance of renewing our mind through time in the word of God to combat the negative thoughts and influence of the world (Romans 12:2).

To conclude this brief look at what the Bible says about mental health, we need to understand how we are to use our healthy mind to do the work of the ministry.

Having a sense of accomplishment in your life goes a long way for your mental health. I am convinced you will never be truly fulfilled in your life unless you are doing what God created you to do for his glory. But if you are working for your own selfish needs, then you will have emptiness in your soul. In the last few years, I have noticed a serious problem that is pervasive in our society. That problem is a desire to not work, coupled with a lack of meaningful relationships with others.

For some time now, I have said we live in a fast-food society. We want everything right now with little to no effort. Frankly, it seems like there are too many people who want things given to them as opposed to working for it. There will always be a greater appreciation for those things that you work for. Even in the sports world, often the athletes who are not the most talented, go further because they have the determination to do what it takes more than the ones who rest on talent alone.

Created for a Purpose

God created us for a purpose. When God made Adam, the first thing he did was place him in the Garden of Eden to dress and keep it.

Genesis 2:15 KJV
And the Lord God took the man, and put him into the garden of Eden to dress it and to keep it.

Now, the garden was well watered and there was no curse on the earth since Adam had not sinned at this point. So the garden would have been easy to take care of. Now the work indeed was probably easy, but still he had work to do. Adam filled a purpose in God's plan. God uses this physical Old Testament example to teach us a spiritual truth. The Lord has a garden or field of ministry that he wants us to work in. That field of ministry could be your family, friends, coworkers, fellow students at school, or people in your neighborhood. There are people all around us that physically and, most importantly, spiritually need to be attended to. They need the Sun of righteousness and the water of the word of God (Malachi 4:2, Ephesians 5:26). The Lord wants to use you to share the truth with others. When you show others how to have a renewed mind, it will help your spirit/mind as well.

Not only is there a lackadaisical attitude to work, there is also the devastating issue of a lack of meaningful relationships with others. Another important truth we see God relates to us through Adam is that it is not good for man to be alone.

Genesis 2:18 KJV
And the Lord God said, It is not good that the man should be alone; I will make him an help meet for him.

Historically and doctrinally the Lord is referring to Adam needing Eve to help him fulfill God's plan. But we also see in general it is not good for any person to be alone. We are social beings. Priority relationship number one is with the Lord and then others after that.

In Jesus' earthly ministry, he had a group of men and women that assisted him in ministry. Jesus is God with skin on but still had his disciples, not only to teach them but help him spread the gospel of the kingdom. Even when he sent his disciples out to preach the gospel, he sent them two by two (Mark 6:7). When you look at the apostle Paul, he rarely worked in ministry alone. He always worked with others to minister the gospel of grace.

Indeed, ministry is all about establishing relationships with people. Those close ministry relationships are good for our mental health.

1 Thessalonians 2:8 KJV
So being affectionately desirous of you, we were willing to have imparted unto you, not the gospel of God only, but also our own souls, because ye were dear unto us.

I think we learned the hard way during the COVID shutdown of 2020 that it is not good for man to be alone. Depression, suicide, and addictive behaviors increased during that time significantly. Our children lost out on so much due to a lack of socialization. Not only was this bad for our society in general, it was detrimental to our churches as they too shut down. The local church is here to help edify and build up one another. The local church is what God uses to show the truth of the gospel of grace to the world. He wants us as believers to work together to minister. It was hard to do that during the shutdown as we were made to not be around others. But now, even three and a half years later, we still have believers that do not foster face-to-face fellowship. They only do church online from the convenience of their home. I am thankful for the technology we have to share the word of God in this fashion. I have members of my church who physically can't make it to the service, so they watch online. But that will never replace the need to have that human contact.

2 John 1:12 KJV
Having many things to write unto you, I would not write with paper and ink: but I trust to come unto you, and speak face to face, that our joy may be full.

Do you know what the common thread is between a successful ministry and a good biblical relationship? The answer is being willing to work at it. Again, anything we do that brings success is going to take work.

After Israel was in captivity for 70 years, they returned to their land and rebuilt the temple. Later, Nehemiah returns to have the walls around Jerusalem rebuilt. They were able to complete the work quickly because they had a mind to work.

Nehemiah 4:6 KJV
So built we the wall; and all the wall was joined together unto the half thereof: for the people had a mind to work.

Whether it is ministry or our relationships with others, if we do not have a mind to work, those ministries and relationships will deteriorate.

Proverbs 24:30-34 KJV
I went by the field of the slothful, and by the vineyard of the man void of understanding; [31] And, lo, it was all grown over with thorns, and nettles had covered the face thereof, and the stone wall thereof was broken down. [32] Then I saw, and considered it well: I looked upon it, and received instruction. [33] Yet a little sleep, a little slumber, a little folding of the hands to sleep: [34] So shall thy poverty come as one that travelleth; and thy want as an armed man.

In the above passage, you have the account of a wise man going by the field of the slothful. The slothful is someone that we would call lazy today. They do not perform the needed work in order to have their field to yield fruit. The end result of the slothful person not willing to do the work is poverty. The wise man looks upon this situation and receives instruction. This is a great example of learning what not to do. We can relate this story to our jobs, ministry, and relationships. We can even relate the above story to our own mental health. In my years in ministry and law enforcement, I have dealt with people that want a better life but are not willing to put in the necessary work to change their situation. In other words they do not have a mind to work. The apostle Paul sums up what we need to do in the following verse:

Romans 12:11 KJV
Not slothful in business; fervent in spirit; serving the Lord;

Having a fervent spirit is having a spirit or mind that has zeal. That is literally opposite of being slothful.

Work of the Ministry

Just like God gave Adam work to do, he has given each and every one of us work to do as well. It is this work that gives us purpose in life, which begins when we accept Jesus Christ as our Lord and Savior. We cannot work our way to heaven. Jesus Christ did all the work for us on the cross. We are saved by his wonderful grace alone. But we are saved to do good works.

Ephesians 2:8-10 KJV
For by grace are ye saved through faith; and that not of your-selves: it is the gift of God: [9] Not of works, lest any man should boast. [10] For we are his workmanship, created in Christ Jesus unto good works, which God hath before ordained that we should walk in them.

2 Timothy 1:9 KJV
Who hath saved us, and called us with an holy calling, not ac-

cording to our works, but according to his own purpose and grace, which was given us in Christ Jesus before the world began,

What's incredible to think about, on both of these above verses, we see God has already ordained or appointed good works for us to walk in even before the world began! God is all-knowing and has a master plan that includes you. If we are not walking in his word fulfilling his purpose in our lives, then we will never feel like we have purpose and meaning. That in itself can leave us depressed and weakened in our mental health.

In a recent sermon, I was talking about this very point. I used an eagle as an example. If you saw an eagle living among chickens and acting like a chicken, you would be dumbfounded. An eagle was made to soar high in the sky and is the top bird among birds. It was not created to peck for food on the ground and not fly. Mentally, that is the problem of a lot of Christians. God created us to soar like eagles, and yet we are acting like chickens. We need to take a step of faith and walk in the good works the Lord has created us to do in Christ. Being obedient to God's purpose and plan for our lives will go a long way in being biblically mentally healthy.

The Need of Biblical Relationships

Again, ministry is about relationships. If we are trying to reach others for Christ, then we need to build a relationship with them in order to share the gospel of grace. If we are discipling another believer in their walk with the Lord, we need to build a relationship with them so we communicate life to others and not just Bible facts. Paul was always concerned about this as he worked with others in ministry. He inquired about how they were doing and he let them know how he was doing. He didn't hide what was going on even when he was in prison for Christ.

He let others know exactly what his state was and he, likewise, wanted to honestly know what's going on in their lives.

Colossians 4:7-9 KJV
All my state shall Tychicus declare unto you, who is a beloved brother, and a faithful minister and fellowservant in the Lord: [8] Whom I have sent unto you for the same purpose, that he might know your estate, and comfort your hearts; [9] With Onesimus, a faithful and beloved brother, who is one of you. They shall make known unto you all things which are done here.

Paul says in the above passage that Tychicus will declare ALL my state. Likewise, Paul wanted to know their estate. This was not a one-sided relationship. It is so important to our mental wellbeing that we have friends who will be willing to listen to us, as well as we need to listen to them.

Even in the trials and tribulations that we go through, which can be mentally taxing, the comfort we receive from the Lord, we need to be ready to turn around and give that same comfort to others.

2 Corinthians 1:3-4 KJV
Blessed be God, even the Father of our Lord Jesus Christ, the Father of mercies, and the God of all comfort; [4] Who comforteth us in all our tribulation, that we may be able to comfort them which are in any trouble, by the comfort wherewith we ourselves are comforted of God.

The Lord will comfort us in all of our tribulations so we can comfort others in any trouble they may have. This comfort of heart and mind or soul and spirit comes from the Spirit of God and the word of God.

John 14:26 KJV

But the Comforter, which is the Holy Ghost, whom the Father will send in my name, he shall teach you all things, and bring all things to your remembrance, whatsoever I have said unto you.

Romans 15:4 KJV

For whatsoever things were written aforetime were written for our learning, that we through patience and comfort of the scriptures might have hope.

We may not go through the exact problem of someone else. But as we receive comfort from God's word in our tribulations, we can share that with others that we minister to. This is why it is so vital for each believer in Christ to have a daily walk with the Lord through his word and prayer. Yes, it will take some work. Being able to minister the word to others takes some effort. We need to take time out of our schedule to spend time in the word and be willing to sacrifice time to spend with others who are in need. That's why it is called the work of the ministry.

Ephesians 4:11-12 KJV

And he gave some, apostles; and some, prophets; and some, evangelists; and some, pastors and teachers; [12] For the perfecting of the saints, for the work of the ministry, for the edifying of the body of Christ:

2 Timothy 2:15 KJV

Study to shew thyself approved unto God, a workman that needeth not to be ashamed, rightly dividing the word of truth.

What the Lord desires for us to do in ministry with and to

others requires that we have a mind to work (Nehemiah 4:6). If we are going to have a mind to work, then we need to renew our own mind daily so we can be spiritually minded and not carnally minded (Romans 12:2, Ephesians 4:23, Romans 8:5-6). There is no doubt that everyone who is lost or saved struggles in their thoughts from time to time. Many face serious mental health issues regularly. The battleground is in the mind and will manifest itself in our actions (2 Corinthians 10:5). Thoughts lead to attitudes, and attitudes lead to actions.

The Lord has given us 66 counselors to help us as we live and serve him in this dark and sinful world. Those 66 counselors are each book in the Bible from Genesis to Revelation. It is the Lord that created us and knows exactly what we need to be mentally healthy (Genesis 1:26, 1 Thessalonians 5:23). It all boils down to committing ourselves to having a daily walk with the Lord in his word. That's how we have the mind of Christ in us (Philippians 2:5).

Psalm 119:24 KJV
Thy testimonies also are my delight and my counsellors.

Conclusion

One thing I have learned in the past year, none of us is immune from having times in our life that we may be mentally weakened. We can simply be sad about a situation or face depression. Maybe we are battling anxiety or even worse, thoughts of suicide. Being a believer in Christ does not shield you from this. But, as believers, we have the ability and means to get back to being mentally healthy through Christ. We have his word and fellow believers in Christ to help heal our minds. As Christians we are commanded to comfort the feeble minded.

1 Thessalonians 5:14 KJV
Now we exhort you, brethren, warn them that are unruly, comfort the feebleminded, support the weak, be patient toward all men.

To be feeble minded is to have a weakened mind. God does not mean for us to stay feeble minded. That is why we see this command to comfort them. That comfort will come from application of the word of God as we have seen throughout this book. Remember, our mental health is also connected with serving and helping others in their walk. So, let us stay mentally healthy together.

Romans 15:4 KJV
For whatsoever things were written aforetime were written for our learning, that we through patience and comfort of the scriptures might have hope.

2 Corinthians 1:3-4 KJV
Blessed be God, even the Father of our Lord Jesus Christ, the Father of mercies, and the God of all comfort; [4] Who comforteth us in all our tribulation, that we may be able to comfort them which are in any trouble, by the comfort wherewith we ourselves are comforted of God.

It is my sincere hope and prayer that everyone that has read this work will indeed have a healthy mind through the mind of Christ each and every day.